D1298594

# THE UNTOLD STORY

## About The War of 1812

*A devastating blow to the American forces occurs in the small town of Essex, Connecticut.*

Enjoy a wee bit of History!

Kajsa C. Cook

KAJSA C. COOK

*AuthorHouse™*
*1663 Liberty Drive*
*Bloomington, IN 47403*
*www.authorhouse.com*
*Phone: 1-800-839-8640*

*©2011 Kajsa C. Cook. All rights reserved.*

*No part of this book may be reproduced, stored in a retrieval system, or transmitted by any means without the written permission of the author.*

*First published by AuthorHouse 2/23/2011*

*ISBN: 9781452065571 (sc)*
*ISBN: 9781452065588 (e)*

*Library of Congress Control Number: 2010917932*

*Printed in the United States of America*

*Any people depicted in stock imagery provided by Thinkstock are models, and such images are being used for illustrative purposes only.*
*Certain stock imagery © Thinkstock.*

*This book is printed on acid-free paper.*

*Because of the dynamic nature of the Internet, any Web addresses or links contained in this book may have changed since publication and may no longer be valid. The views expressed in this work are solely those of the author and do not necessarily reflect the views of the publisher, and the publisher hereby disclaims any responsibility for them.*

# Acknowledgments

Thanks to my good friend, Mary Margaret Stewart. Her help and enthusiasm encouraged me to write this book.

This marker is located in the Essex town park telling the history of the town.

# Introduction

Almost 1000 U.S. ships had been seized by France and Great Britain between 1807 and 1812. They had also placed restrictions on U.S. trade. Great Britain would board U.S. ships, impress the seamen and force them into service for the British Royal Navy.

New England was against the war. It hurt the trade and most of the seamen impressed by the British were from New England. Connecticut would not send soldiers into battle.

President James Madison declared war on June 18th, 1812. This was a big risk, for if the U.S. was defeated, we could lose our independence forever. At the time of the war, the navy had few ships, the army was small, and Britain had one of the world's greatest fighting forces.

Some call The War of 1812, the second war for independence.

Little is written about the British raid on Essex, Connecticut, but it was a devastating blow to our country. Twenty-eight ships were destroyed in the shipyards of this small town located six miles up the Connecticut River.

# Contents

# APRIL 1813
# Chapter 1

## GRANDFATHER SAVES THE DAY

Why is it that when you can sleep late, you wake up anyway? Austin lay there thinking about this but then decided he had better things to do. He gazed out the small window directly opposite his bed. Another day was about to begin; no longer was the sky dark, now it was grey with streaks of pink and lavender. He and his brother Nathan shared the bed in a small room in the attic. In winter it was freezing and in summer it was so hot, the two of them often slept on a blanket outside. The best place was under the large oak tree near the back porch. And of course it was near the kitchen. Many a night they would raid the cupboard, grabbing some bread and preserves and then tiptoe outside again, trying not to giggle. They certainly didn't want to wake up their father.

Austin checked to see if Nate was awake. Deliberately he kicked him. Nate snorted and turned over.

"Wake up!" Again Austin kicked him.

"Wha, what do you want? Stop kicking me," Nate growled. Suddenly he sat up. "When did you and Grandfather get home last night? Did you catch plenty of cod?"

"Well, if you hadn't been such a sleepy head, I would have told you last night what happened. Bet you would really have liked to be with us." Austin knew he had Nate's attention. "Well, first we did catch plenty of fish. We sailed almost to Long Island. We saw a couple of sharks and they had discovered a school of fish. Grandfather said when they had their fill they would swim away and then we could catch as many fish as we needed. So anyway, there we were busy spilling the fish out of the net into the hold, when it happened."

"What happened, Austin? Hurry up. Tell me."

Austin sat up and pulled his knees up to his chest and rested his elbows. He was so excited he could barely talk.

"Nate, you would have been so scared! Just as we were dumping the last of the fish in our boat, I looked up and coming right at us was an English brig. I yelled at grandfather, 'There's an English brig off the starboard. Look, they're coming right at us. Do you think they see us?'

'Yep they sure do, but I don't think they saw you because you were leaning over the net. Austin, cover yourself with the net so they won't see you. I don't want them to impress you into their Navy. They'll see I'm too old. They won't want me but you're just what they are looking for, so don't move and stay quiet.' "I did just what he said and I could hear the ship coming closer. Then the captain was yelling to grandfather. I couldn't see him but this is what he was yelling. 'Old man, what do you have there? Looks like a good catch of fish.' He turned to his first mate. 'Take the long boat and go get that old man's fish. He's too old for us but not his catch. By jove, they are fresh.'

"And then Nate, that mate got into our boat and grabbed grandfather by the throat and shook him and forced him to sit down. And guess where he sat? On top of the net! Then the mate started to put as many fish as he could into bags he had with him. He then gave grandfather a kick in the belly, jumped into his boat with our fish, and rowed away."

"Doggone, Austin, you were sure lucky that the British didn't find you. Sure as shoot'in, you'd be taken to their ship and we'd never see you again, just like those men from Saybrook."

"Yep, I was sure lucky. That whole crew was impressed by the British. They said they were looking for deserters, so they took everyone except the captain and his mates. I was lucky, too, because when grandfather sat on me, he didn't squish me." Austin chuckled. "But he sure was heavy. Come on, Let's get dressed. I'm hungry."

As they ran down the steps, they almost knocked over their sisters, Beth and Mary. Beth was a year older than Austin, so she figured she could scold her younger brothers. "You know mother expects you two to behave."

"Don't worry, we will. You know Beth, you sound just like mother." Austin grinned. Beth scowled. While

Austin and Beth were whispering to each other, Nate and Mary dodged around them and raced down the stairs.

Their mother was busy stirring the porridge and making sure the ham on the spit didn't get scorched. Grandfather had gotten up early, brought in more firewood, and was already enjoying his breakfast. "Well, look who's here. It's about time you came downstairs for breakfast. Ah, here's Austin. I take it you're none the worse for our adventure. When I was forced to sit on you, I thought you might make a noise, but you were very brave." He chuckled. "After all I'm not a small man!"

Nate scrambled onto the bench where the children sat, and reached for his cup of milk. "Grandfather, Austin told me all about the British ship and what happened. Did the British hurt you?"

"Nope, I'm a tough old man."

The back door slammed and Mr. Lay, Austin's father, walked in carrying two buckets of fresh milk. The Lays lived a short way outside of town and owned a few acres. They had several cows, two horses and many chickens. They also had one ferocious rooster that enjoyed chasing every one that came near him. In the back yard, there was a large vegetable garden and the chicken coop. It was Beth and Mary's chores to collect the eggs, clean the chicken coop, and help their mother plant and weed the vegetable garden.

Beyond the yard was the pasture. Every day Austin and Nathan carried buckets of water from the well to the trough used by both cows and horses.

When the morning chores were finished, Mr. Lay and

Austin walked to the shipyard where they both worked. Austin's father was a skilled shipbuilder. Austin no longer attended school. He was glad that his father had decided that he was old enough to earn a living. Austin was his father's apprentice and hoped he would become as skilled as his father some day.

The shipyard was really busy these days. The men worked long hours getting the ships ready to go to war. There was a constant sound of hammers and saws. The ships ready to sail were docked in the harbor. Others were almost finished except for painting. That was a job that Austin enjoyed. When a ship had been painted, and ready to launch, it was beautiful, and to Austin, it seemed each ship was restless and couldn't wait to sink its hull into the water.

Austin enjoyed working with his father and knew the other shipyard workers considered his father one of the best. When it was time for lunch, the men gathered under the big oak tree, ate their lunch and talked of the war. Austin could hardly wait for lunchtime to tell everyone what had happened to him and his grandfather. He gobbled down his sandwich and stood up. As he told yesterday's adventure, he was so excited, he almost stuttered.

Most of the men had friends and relatives who spent most of their lives on the water as fishermen or traders. And they all knew men and boys who had been impressed by the British navy.

Wilbur Cooper was one of Mr. Lay's friends. "Sure was lucky that your grandfather made you hide. You're thirteen, right? The British would have loved to get their hands on you."

"Know what makes me mad about the British?" said Mr. Lay angrily. There're trying to take over the ocean. They don't want us trading with any country in Europe or the Carribean. The whole coastline is blockaded.

"Well, we started the war, and here we are fighting on the seas with so few ships against the British Navy. The good thing is that the British are fighting in Europe and they don't have as many ships as they would like to fight against us. The Revolutionary War ended in 1783 and now we're fighting the second war for independence," grumbled Wilbur. "We'll sure have to win this war, too, and then it will be the end of "Merry Old England" interfering in our affairs."

"When did the war start, Father? I know it was last year some time." Austin wanted to know.

"To be exact, we declared war on June 18,1812. Don't you remember the battle between the USS CONSTITUTION and HMS GUERRIERE? They fought last August. The whole battle was written up in The SPECTATOR and I remember it well. Our ship won!" Mr. Lay nodded his head in satisfaction. "The CONSTITUTION was chased for three days by five British ships, but the captain was able to lose them and sailed into Boston harbor. And then on August 19th, the CONSTITUTION saw the GUERRIERE all by itself. Didn't have four other ships to help this time. And so Captain Isaac Hull won. The GUERRIERE was wrecked. It was burned after removing the wounded, and the rest of the crew were imprisoned. Sure would have liked to have been there to see that."

Amos Smith spoke. He was a young man who worked with Wilbur Cooper as his apprentice. "I remember that too. I save all the war news in the paper." He looked around at all the men. He wanted them to see how smart he was.

Austin had finished eating. Since his adventure with the British and after listening to the others, he decided he could speak. He stood up and said excitedly, "If the war lasts long enough, I'm going to join our navy and fight those British."

"No you won't young man," said his father. "We need you here to build more ships."

Dejected, Austin turned and went back to work.

# CHAPTER 2

# A DAY AT THE SHORE

Several weeks had passed. It had been a busy time for all the Lays. The vegetable garden was flourishing; one of their cows had a calf, and Mr. Lay and Austin were proud to say another ship was ready to launch.

It was a warm sunny day and Mrs. Lay had been looking forward to visiting her friend Carrie Larson for some time. "Your father knows, Austin, that I've decided to go to Saybrook so we can visit with the Larson family." The Larson family lived close to Long Island Sound on a small farm. "You don't have to work at the shipyard today so get the wagon ready. Make sure it's clean and put a couple of blankets where we'll be sitting. Don't want any splinters. Nathan can help you harness the horses and the girls will fix a nice lunch. If Mrs. Larson isn't too busy, we can mosey down to the shore and have our picnic there." Mrs. Lay patted Austin on the back. "You can all go wading."

Austin yelled. "Hey everybody, we're going to Saybrook and go wading. Hurry up."

Nate was on the back porch collecting firewood for the stove. "I'm ready, I'm ready," he called, almost dropping the wood. He hurried inside and after putting the wood next to the stove, grabbed Austin by the arm. "Come on, Austin, let's get the wagon ready." He was half way to the barn before Austin was out the door.

Beth and Mary ran into the kitchen. "I heard what you were saying to Austin, Ma, and we're ready to go," said Beth, as she started wrapping slices of ham. "I sure hope Mrs. Larson can go with us and Becky, Sam and Anne. They are so lucky to live right near the Sound. I'll be so glad to see Becky. Ma, what do you think about asking her mother if Becky can come for a visit?"

"Well I suppose I can ask." Mrs. Lay was already carrying a basket outside.

Mary piped up. "I want to go wading and I can play with Anne." She skipped around the table and out the door.

Soon they were ready to go. Mr. Lay waved goodbye. "Have a good time, but Austin, go easy. I don't want you to race the horses. Don't forget," he yelled as the wagon turned the corner and they were on their way. Austin nodded and waved to his father. As if these ole horses could go fast, Austin grumbled to himself.

It didn't take very long to travel the six miles to the Larson's home. Sam was pumping water from the well when they arrived. Mrs. Larson was hanging clothes in the back yard. "Hey Ma, the Lays are here," shouted Sam.

Nathan and Austin jumped down and tied the horses to the hitching post.

"Morning to you," called Mrs. Larson from the back yard. She came running to greet the Lay family. "Come in, come in. Landsakes, I haven't seen you for quite a spell." She was all smiles as she and Mrs. Lay walked arm in arm to the house. "I baked a cake this morning. Must have known I'd have company." She laughed. "Oh, I'm so glad to see you."

The children took their cake outside and the two women now had a chance to talk. "Carrie. What do you hear from your husband? Is he still on the frigate, NEVLIN?" Mrs. Lay asked as she sipped her coffee.

Her friend burst into tears. "I don't know. He was on the ship, but the British boarded her and impressed the crew. I don't know where he is or if I'll ever see him again."

"Well, worrying about him won't help. You can't do anything about it and you'll just make yourself miserable and the children, too." Mrs. Lay patted her friend's shoulder. "We came to visit you, and the children want to go wading in the Sound. We brought a picnic lunch and hoped you could come with us. It's such a beautiful day and you need to take some time to just relax. I know how you work."

Mrs. Larson wiped her face, blew her nose and smiled at Mrs. Lay. "You're right, I need to take a day off and just enjoy it. All I need to do is hang out the last basket of clothes and I'll be ready."

Austin had unharnessed the horses and led them into the Larson pasture with Sam's help. Everyone helped hang Mrs. Larson's laundry and very soon they were ready. It was a short walk to the beach from the Larson's home.

Austin, Nate, and Sam had their boots off, their pants rolled up and were already splashing each other before the girls had even set the lunch basket on a flat rock. Waves splashed against large boulders and the rocky shore was rough on bare feet. Finally the girls were ready. They had removed their heavy shoes and hiked up their skirts. They gingerly made their way across the stones and dipped their toes in the water. That was enough for them. The water was still cold. Becky had waded farther than the other girls and turned to carefully wade back to the shore. Austin saw her begin to fall on the slippery rocks, and grabbed her hand. He was thrilled to be able to help her because he wouldn't have dared to hold her hand, but this was different. He had always thought Becky was special.

"Thanks so much Austin, for helping me. If I had fallen, I'd be soaked, so you saved me." Becky smiled at him.

He helped her over the rocks still holding her hand, until Nate, seeing his brother holding hands with Becky, began to splash them both. "Austin likes Becky. Austin likes Becky," he chanted. Disgusted with his brother and red in the face, Austin splashed him back, until they were both soaked.

In the meantime, Becky was helping Beth and Mary with the lunch. "Never mind about Nate," said Beth. "He thinks he's funny. Wait until he gets older and likes a girl. We'll really tease him."

Becky could feel her face getting red. "Oh dear, I think my face must be getting red. I must have been in the sun too long." She didn't want Beth to think she was blushing. But she was glad that maybe Austin did like her.

It had been a lovely special day. Everyone had enjoyed the lunch and not having to work for a whole day was a rare treat.

As they trudged back to the Larson's home, the two mothers lagged behind. "It's been so difficult since my husband isn't here." Mrs. Larson sighed. "I decided that Becky is old enough to work and she has a position with the Pratt family that live not far from you. I was wondering if she could visit you when she has her half day off. She and Beth are such good friends, I know they will enjoy seeing each other, and looks to me like Austin might enjoy seeing her as well." She winked.

"Of course, dear friend, we'll be happy to see her whenever she can get away. I think she'll enjoy working for the Pratt family. They are a very important family in town and also very kind." Mrs. Lay smiled. "I think you're right about Austin. I've seen him look at Rebecca, but he's so shy. Oh well, they're much too young to have special feelings, but they can enjoy a friendship."

# CHAPTER 3

# THE SHIPYARD

The shipyard was busy from sunrise to sunset. Every man felt responsible for building as many ships as possible. Austin felt a glow of pride seeing the ships he and his father had helped build. Some were already launched and anchored in the cove. Austin had done much of the painting, and helped with all the ropes needed on the decks. Already the hull of the next ship was completed and he and his father would be working on that ship in the next week.

"Here comes Nate with our lunch, Pa, and I'm starved." Austin yelled to his father. It didn't take very long before all the men had stopped working, grabbed their lunches, and found their special spot in the shade where they could enjoy their lunch. As they ate, the talk turned to war as usual.

Some of the men weren't able to read and depended on the young men to tell them what had happened. The local paper, SPECTATOR, was usually behind in the news. That really didn't matter to the men as long as the news was read out loud to them so they'd know what was happening.

Wilbur Cooper had listened quietly while Amos read the news. "By the way," he said, "Jonathon Walker is back home after nearly being killed up near Canada. Had a chance to talk to him. You know he lost an arm. He was fighting an Indian who wanted his scalp. Well, Jonathon wasn't about to let that happen. They were fighting and the Indian almost chopped his arm off with his tomahawk. Just then one of Jonathon's officers saw what was happening and shot the Indian. Then he put Jonathon's belt above the wound to stop the bleeding. By then Jonathon had fainted dead away. There weren't no doctors, so some of his buddies carried him to a safe place and laid him there. Sure is a wonder he lived, 'cause they had to cut off his arm and then used a branding iron to cauterize the wound. He don't remember a thing about it. Just as well, but now he's home. He was fighting with General Hull's troops. They were planning to invade Canada. I think he was near Lake Erie when the British and the Indians attacked."

"Yep, I remember about that battle." Austin's father took a big swallow of water. "There was a big story about it in the Middletown paper. General Hull fought in the Revolutionary War and guess he's pretty old by now. Anyway, he got scared when some of his men were attacked by Indians so he retreated back to Fort Detroit. Guess most of his men thought he was a coward but maybe he just lost his nerve. Probably won't be the last we hear of him."

"Nope, we haven't heard the last of him, but did you know that Captain Isaac Hull is his nephew? You know who I mean. He commands the USS Constitution." Wilbur Cooper tapped his pipe on the bench and carefully put his empty pipe in his pocket. "Come on, you young lads, can't just sit there and look at the rest of us. We'd better get back to work."

The thoughts of war filled Austin's head. Well, if I was allowed to go to war, I'd rather join the navy. Don't want some Indian using his hatchet on me. Wonder if I look old enough to run away and join the navy. Father says I'm needed here but sure isn't as exciting as fighting the British. Austin sighed. Guess I'll just have to wait awhile and see what happens.

That evening when the family was sitting around the table having their dinner, Grandfather had his chance to speak. "Ever since the British took my catch when Austin and me were out in the sound, I've done my fishing in the river. But I'm thinking about taking a trip up the river, maybe to Hartford. I'd like Austin to go with me. Can you do without him, son, for a couple of days? I know you're real busy at the boat yard."

"I guess we could manage without Austin for awhile." His father winked at him.

Austin looked from his father to his grandfather. "You mean I can go with Grandfather?" His father chuckled. "Yep, you may as well. You've never been to Hartford so this is a good chance for you to enjoy a couple of days."

Father smiled at him. "Besides, your mother can make a list of supplies she needs from there. You can pick them up. It sure saves me a trip with the wagon, and would take much longer. With sails and oars, you'll do just fine."

"Austin, that will really help all of us." His mother laughed. "Just think, Austin, you'll have two skills, so when you grow up, you can decide to either build ships or sail them."

Austin grinned. He was so excited. It would be so much fun to spend a couple of days with grandfather and also see Hartford. "What's Hartford like, Grandfather? Has to be a lot bigger than here. Where will we stay? Can we eat somewhere? Where will we buy all the supplies on the list?"

His thoughts were racing and he could hardly get his words out without shouting.

"Why can't I go," Nate interrupted. "Maybe I'm younger than Austin, but I'm real strong, and bet I could row all the way to Hartford."

"Now Nathan, none of that complaining. You can't go. We need you here to help with the chores and besides you are too young. Wait a couple of years and then grandfather will take you." Mrs. Lay spoke firmly and Nate knew she meant business. He put his elbows on the table and scowled.

"Now, can I answer Austin's questions," Grandfather frowned at Nate. "First, yep, It's bigger than here, which is why your mother wants us to pick up supplies. Plenty more shops and lots more people. There are some good places to eat a hearty meal, and we can sleep overnight in the skiff. Now, that's enough questions. I'm tired and I'm going to bed."

It was getting late and by now the whole family was exhausted. Once all the chores were finished, it wasn't long before they were all in bed.

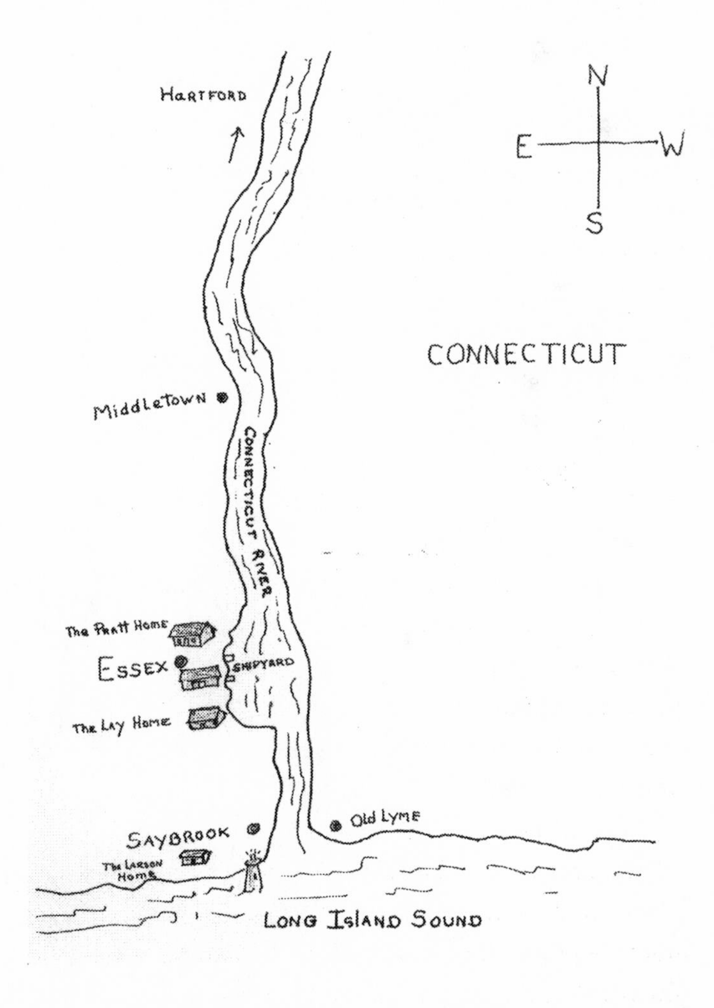

# CHAPTER 4

# A SURPRISING EVENT

Everyone was sleeping except Austin. He kept thinking about traveling up the river and then imagining what it would be like to see Hartford. There would be all kinds of shops and people driving through town with beautiful horses pulling their fancy carriages. Bet just about everybody was rich. It was exciting to think about. He tossed and turned until his pillow was on the floor. Rolling over and picking up his pillow, he turned to look at Nathan. Did he wake him up? Nope, Nathan was still sound asleep, so he hadn't been bothered by Austin's tossing and kicking.

Two weeks had passed since the family had talked about Grandfather and Austin going to Hartford up the Connecticut River in their skiff. Now the day had arrived. Carefully, Austin slipped out of bed and quickly dressed. It didn't take him very long to tiptoe down the stairs. His knapsack was packed with a change of clothing and when he walked into the kitchen, he saw the packet his mother had prepared of food, and he stuffed that into his knapsack. So now he was ready but where was grandfather? Ah, here he's coming through the back door.

"Morn'in Austin, are you ready? I checked the skiff and all is in good shape. No sense in waking everyone, so bring your knapsack and we'll be on our way." Grandfather started toward the door when he turned and asked. "What did you do with the food your mother packed?"

"Oh, I saw it on the kitchen table and I put it in my knapsack," Austin replied.

Dawn had arrived and the early morning sun made the water sparkle. It was going to be a beautiful day. Austin put everything in the small cabin, untied the rope while his grandfather prepared the sails. Soon they were on their way. There was a good breeze and the small craft danced merrily over the water.

"If the wind keeps up, it won't be long before we get to Hartford." Austin grinned at grandfather.

"Doubt if the wind keeps up," Grandfather replied. "We're sailing against the current. Mind you, we'll be using the oars most of the way. Now coming back, it's going to be easier because we'll be going with the current. Won't take as long. Your arms better be real strong." Grandfather winked at Austin.

It was so peaceful. Not many boats were going up or down the river so early in the day. Austin had plenty of time to look at the houses, farms and pastures as they sailed passed. In one pasture a young lad was leading his cows from the barn and waved to Austin.

The sun was getting higher in the sky. The wind had stopped and the water was calm.

"Well, Austin, guess you'll have to start rowing and use those strong muscles. But don't worry we'll take turns because we have a long way to go. You row while I take down the sail."

"Aw, Grandfather, we didn't have breakfast yet. Can we tie up someplace and eat something? I'm so durn hungry and I know Mother packed us plenty of food."

Grandfather nodded. "Row over to the bank on the right. See that tree close to the water? Aim for that and when we get close enough, jump out and tie the rope around it."

Austin grabbed the rope and waded to the bank. He tied the rope around the tree and made sure he had tied it with a strong knot. Grandfather waded to the bank carrying the packet of food he had grabbed from Austin's knapsack. It was a good spot. There were plenty of trees and some boulders where they could sit.

"We can't stay very long, Austin. I want to get to Hartford and get everything on the list this afternoon. We'll sleep on the boat tonight and leave at dawn tomorrow." Grandfather suddenly looked up. He had been checking his pockets for his tobacco. "I hear something, Austin. Sounds like it's coming from over there beyond those trees."

"Probably an old cow. I'll go look." Austin headed for the trees. He was curious to know what he would find. Just then he saw a movement behind some of the bushes and heard a muffled cough. He stopped in his tracks. That sure wasn't any ole cow, that's a person. Who could be hiding?

Suddenly a head appeared. Why, it was a boy about his age.

"Hey, what are you doing? Why are you hiding?" Austin wasn't scared now that he saw the boy. He figured he wasn't going to harm his grandfather or himself. "Come over here," he called, "what's your name and why are you hiding?"

Slowly the boy crawled out from behind the bushes. His clothes were torn to shreds and he was so skinny he had a frayed piece of rope holding up his pants, what there was of them. He had brown shaggy hair and was about as tall as Austin.

"I saw you tie your boat to that tree and then you were eating some food. I'm so hungry, I just had to watch you eat. I'm on my way to Hartford where I live. Been walking for days ever since I left Boston. My name's Joshua and I'd surely appreciate some food if you can spare it."

"Aw, come on, we have an extra boiled egg and some ham you can have. Come meet my grandfather." Austin felt sorry for Joshua and couldn't imagine being so hungry and so far away from home.

"Well there, son, heard you say you were hungry. Set down and eat." Grandfather handed Joshua the egg and ham. He wolfed it down so fast he must have been starving.

"That was sure good and thank you kindly. Well, guess I'd better be on my way", he said, as he was getting up to leave.

"Now, just one minute, young man, not so fast. I want to know why you were hiding and why you look half starved." Grandfather lit his pipe and looked intently at Joshua.

Joshua sat down again. "Well, guess I've always wanted to see the ocean, so about a year ago, I left Hartford and after a heap of walking, I finally arrived in Boston. Took me a while to look around, but I wanted to work on a ship so finally got a job on a frigate. We sailed out of the harbor and had to be real careful because of the British blockade, but we managed to slip through at nighttime. We were on our way to the Carribean to pick up cargo when a British warship saw us. We got captured and our crew was taken on board their ship. The Captain said we were all British subjects and so he impressed us. I tell you, by then I was feeling pretty low. They worked us as hard as they could and we didn't get much food either. If we were too slow doing what the first mate told us to do, we got whipped. Guess I'll always have scars on my back. I felt so hopeless. Thought I'd never get home again and my family would think I died. Then one day about a month ago, we sailed up the coast towards Maine. The crew was getting restless. They started complaining because they didn't have any fresh fruit or vegetables. They figured if they anchored close enough to land to use a long boat they could steal from the farmers. The Captain gave orders to anchor closer to land, and so six of their crew started rowing to shore, just when the sun was setting. Well, I'm a good swimmer so I waited until it was dark and then climbed down a rope and slipped into the water. Nobody paid any attention, so I started swimming to shore. Found myself in lots of woods, which was good because I could hide if I had to. Then I started walking south. Finally got to Boston and worked for some lady for a couple of days. She gave me food and let me sleep in her barn. But I've been on the road ever since and have slept in fields most of the time. I'm pretty sure this is the Connecticut River, so I'm going west until I get to Hartford. I'll sure surprise my family."

"It's mighty hard to be impressed by the British. You have had a terrible time but glad you escaped and are on the last part of your journey." Grandfather puffed on his pipe and then stood up. "Austin, what do you say? Shall we take Joshua along to Hartford?"

Austin clapped Joshua's shoulder. "Yep, think we should, Grandfather."

It was getting harder to row, but now there were three to take turns. By the time they reached Hartford it was late afternoon. They were all tired, but happy just to tie up to the wharf and get on land to stretch their aching muscles.

"We have to buy everything on the list, Austin, so we'd better get started before the shops close," Grandfather commented. "Joshua, can you get home from here?"

"I only live down there." Joshua pointed to some dilapidated shacks they could see along the river. "Sure do appreciate your help and golly, will my mother be happy to see me." He shook hands with Grandfather and Austin. He began to hurry along the path that would bring him home. He turned and waved and then he was gone.

Grandfather put his arm around Austin's shoulder. "Bet you're glad the British didn't find you under the net. They were too interested in my catch to see anything unusual. Now you see what they do to young boys they impress."

Austin shuddered. "I sure am glad. Poor Joshua. It must have been terrible to be on that British ship. Glad we could help him and guess he won't be trying to go asailing anymore."

"I think you're right, Austin." Grandfather chuckled. "Best we be on our way."

They finally bought everything on the list. Food supplies came first- flour, sugar, salt and all essentials, as well as everything on father's list. Austin wandered along the aisles and saw candy on a shelf. He had saved some pennies and decided to buy some for Nathan, his sisters, and naturally himself. Maybe I'll buy some for Becky, too, he thought. It would be a good reason to go visit her. Now that she was living at the Platt's home she was living only a half mile away. The Platt house was right in the center of town.

They stored their purchases on board the skiff and then

walked back through town. Grandfather knew of a tavern where they could find fresh seafood. After a delicious dinner of clam chowder and lobster, it was getting late. They settled down on the boat and before Austin knew it, another day had begun. They were on their way early. It was easier going now that the current helped. Finally they were home. Austin could hardly wait to tell everyone about finding Joshua.

While they were eating dinner, Austin told them all about Joshua, the trip to Hartford, the best lobster meal he ever had, and all the shops he had seen.

Austin was anxious to walk to the Pratt house. As soon as the kitchen was in order and he had carried in several buckets of water, he was ready to leave. He didn't want to tell the family where he was going. He knew they would tease him about Becky, especially Nate. Just as he was trying to figure out what excuse to use, his mother said, "Austin, carry this basket of vegetables to Mrs. Pratt.

I promised I would give Mrs. Pratt some from our garden."

"Sure I can do that for you, Ma." What a relief. Now he didn't have to think of an excuse.

It was a lovely evening; a soft breeze was gently swaying the leaves on the trees. When Austin arrived at the Pratt's home, he followed the path around the house to the back door, hoping that Becky would be in the kitchen alone. He peered in the window, and he could see her. She had just finished washing the supper dishes. He rapped lightly on the door and could see her hanging up wet dishtowels. And then the door was opened and Becky was standing there in front of him.

"Austin, what a surprise to see you. I just finished the dishes and I like to sit on the porch and cool off. Do you want to sit on the porch with me for a bit?"

"Don't mind if I do. Becky, this basket of vegetables is from my mother." He cleared his throat. "And here is something for you." He placed the packet of candy on the step beside her. "Go on, open it."

"Oh Austin, how thoughtful of you. Taffy, my favorite candy. Let's have some now. Where did you get it?" As they chewed contently, he told her all about the last two days.

Becky listened intently. She felt sorry for Joshua but glad he was at last home with his family. "You sure had an exciting time. It must have been so wonderful to see Hartford. Someday I'm going there."

"Maybe we can go together." Austin smiled shyly. "Well, guess I'd better be getting home." He brushed off the seat of his pants and waved goodby. He whistled all the way home.

# CHAPTER 5

## BACK TO WORK

It was the next day and the men had stopped work to eat their lunch in their favorite spot under the large oak tree. Austin had been telling them about the adventures he and his grandfather had experienced traveling to Hartford.

"This boy, Joshua, you say was impressed by a British ship? Wonder what happened to the rest of the crew when the Captain discovered one of his American captives had disappeared?" Mr. Cooper was saying as he chewed his slice of bread.

Mr. Lay answered. "He probably thought he fell overboard and drowned. That happens pretty often. By the way, have you heard about the battle of York in Canada? I brought the paper along. Austin, how about reading it to us. Guess it happened a couple of weeks ago. You know how late we get the war news," he grumbled.

Wilbur grabbed the paper and handed it to Austin.

"Sure I'll read it." The war news was on the front page. "Here's what it says."

*During March and April of this year, The Americans collected about 4000 men. On April 26, there were fifteen vessels ready for battle. Many of the men were sick with pneumonia. But they were ready when they finally clashed with the British. They rushed forward and soon forced the British back to the western battery where an open magazine was suddenly detonated by a careless gunner and bodies were blown into the air. This is an incident witnessed by a young boy, Patrick Finan who saw them blown into the air.*

Austin paused. "This is what that boy said."

*A more afflicting sight could scarcely be witnessed... One man in particular presented an awful spectacle; he was brought in a wheelbarrow, and from his appearance I should be inclined to suppose that almost every bone in his body was broken; he was lying in a powerless heap, shaking with every motion of the barrow, from which his legs hung dangling down, as if only connected with his body by the skin, while his cries and groans were of the most heartrending description.*

Austin paused and looked up. "That's really terrible. Can you imagine seeing that poor man? After he paused again, he said quietly, "Well I'll continue reading."

"Wait, young feller, Where did this here battle take place? Don't reckon I know, except it wasn't in the ocean. But since there were vessels taking part, had to be near water." He nodded his head. He was one of the oldest men still working at the shipyard.

"By gum, you're right. Had to be on one of the Great Lakes. Who knows which one?" Wilbur slapped his knee and looked around at the others.

"It was Lake Ontario where that battle took place," said Amos Smith, Wilbur Cooper's apprentice. "You know, in Canada, he said rather smugly.

"Let me finish reading this news." Austin hadn't liked being interrupted but he hadn't been sure either where the battle had taken place. He began to read the rest of the article.

*The British Major General Shaeff, decided to retreat, but left a British flag over their fort to make the Americans think it was still strongly held. He then ordered the "Grand Magazine" blown up.*

*Huge rocks from the explosion landed among townfolk and the Americans. Many were killed or wounded. The Americans did win the battle but discipline broke down and many empty houses were robbed. The Parliament house was set on fire as well as the other public buildings. They also seized a goodly amount of naval stores.*

When Austin had finished, the men were shaking their heads. "Just don't seem right. All those people killed who weren't even soldiers," commented Wilbur Cooper. "Sure wish this dang war was over."

It was time to get back to work. Mr. Lay waited until the others had walked away. "Wilbur, wait," he whispered. "Look, do you see that man walking past? I've seen him a couple of times just walking slowly back and forth on the road. He ties his horse over at the Bushnell tavern."

"Yep, I wondered about him myself. He looks kinda sneaky. In fact, saw him one time writing something while he was looking over here at the boatyard. I think I recognize him. Seems to me he comes from Saybrook."

"Well, I don't like the way he acts. Let's keep an eye on him," Mr. Lay muttered. "Maybe we can find out what he's doing here in our town."

# CHAPTER 6

## AUTUMN DAYS-1813

"Every day is the same," complained Austin as he and his father trudged home after work. Summer was almost over, and the leaves were beginning to turn all the brilliant colors they would wear through the fall.

"Well, Austin, that's life. Some say it's work, eat, sleep, work. And once you start working, it will be most of your life, so hope you find a job that will give you pride in your work and happiness too. Then you won't be complaining. Besides, when you have a family, it brings a lot of joy to your life." His father winked at Austin.

"Yes, but can anyone be happy with this war being fought? I find it hard to imagine what it must be like to see men badly wounded or who have died. And they are men who have fought beside you and have become friends. Sometimes I wish I were old enough to fight, but then I couldn't help to build the ships and that's important."

His father patted his shoulder. He was glad Austin was too young to fight. It was very satisfying to work with

Austin. He had turned out to be a good steady worker. Each day the work continued on the ships and gradually more completed ships were ready to fight. "Austin, you do a fine job. All the men agree and I'm proud of you."

He turned to his father with a big grin. "Did the men really say that?"

"Yep, they sure did. Let's hurry up. Your mother probably has dinner ready and I'm hungry."

When they arrived home, Austin's mother had supper ready. They had fresh tomatoes and corn from their garden and fried fish. Just as the family was ready to sit down, grandfather strolled in with a newspaper rolled up under his arm.

"You'll like the fish we're having. Just caught it this afternoon so it's mighty fresh. Bought a newspaper so guess you'll have to read it to us, Austin, when we're finished with this good supper your lovely mother cooked."

"Now, Grandfather, what do you want from me?" Mrs. Lay knew that grandfather's compliments always meant he wanted something.

"My dear, I just figured that the apples were ripe and sure could enjoy an apple pie."

"Well, that's exactly what we're having for dessert. You old codger, you knew, didn't you?" she said affectionately.

Grandfather chortled. "I just happened to walk into the pantry by mistake and there it was, just waiting to be eaten." He smacked his lips and grinned at her.

The family enjoyed the delicious pie and Grandfather and Nate each decided one piece wasn't quite enough, and persuaded Austin's mother to cut them one more piece. After the dishes were washed and put away, the family returned to the table to hear the news. Austin had been reading to himself, but now he began to read out loud.

"Can't you just tell us what's in the newspaper, Austin? When you read to us, it takes too long," complained Nathan.

"You mean you just want the important facts? Well, I guess I can do that." Austin glanced around the table. They were all ready to listen. He cleared his throat, glanced at the headlines, and began to tell them the war news. "Most of the news is about Commander Oliver Perry. He really outfoxed the British. All through the winter and spring he started a ship building program while they were staying at Presque Isle. So now he had nine vessels ready to attack the British."

"Listen to this," exclaimed Austin. "There was a sand bar between the harbor and Lake Erie. And the British didn't bother to keep up a blockade. They didn't think the Americans could launch the ships over the sand bar. So Commander Perry was smart. They were able to drag the ships across the sand bar."

"That's sure good thinking." Grandfather lit his pipe and thumped Austin on the back. "Go on Austin, then what happened?"

"Well, the Americans fought the British and they won! Let's see. The ship, LAWRENCE was Perry's flagship and was damaged, but Perry managed to board another ship and continue fighting. Sure glad we won," said Austin looking at his father.

"Yep, me too. We need to win more battles and then the British will leave us alone."

"Go back where you came from," chanted Nate, running around the table. "You British!"

"Stop right now, Nathan," scolded his mother. "It's getting dark earlier every day, so light your candles and get ready for bed. Off you go."

The next couple of weeks were busy. Mrs. Lay and the girls were canning the fruit and vegetables from the garden. Mr. Lay and Austin were working at the shipyard every day except Sundays. That left Grandfather and Nate to keep the animals fed and watered. Nate was attending school, not that it made him very happy. When he came home, he would practice reading out loud to grandfather.

"Not bad Nate. You're getting to read real good. Pretty soon you'll be able to read the newspapers to us just like Austin can."

Sunday was a day of rest and only the necessary chores were done. The family went to church in the morning and again in the evening. Everyone at church always sat in the same pew. The Pratt's pew was several pews in front of the Lay's pew. When Becky had a chance, she would come with the Pratt's and Austin had the satisfaction of watching her. He tried to be sneaky about it because Beth sat on one side of him and Nate on the other side. He knew they would tease him if they saw him looking at her too often.

One Sunday evening, Mr. and Mrs. Lay were unable to attend the church service. The children were sent and told to behave themselves. When the service was over, Austin managed to walk next to Becky as they left the church.

"Hi Becky," he whispered so no one else could hear him, "Do you think you can go on a picnic with me next Sunday afternoon?"

"Oh, that sure would be fun. I haven't done very much on my afternoons off, other than go to Saybrook to visit my mother, so yes, I'd like that." She was whispering, too.

As they ambled along, he could see the others way up ahead. Nate was telling them to hurry up. The children were anxious to get home because a freshly baked pie was just waiting to be eaten. Their mother had told them they could have a piece of pie when they returned from church. Now he had a chance to walk Becky to the Pratt's home.

"How is your mother, Becky? Have you heard anything about your father?" It had been many months since her father had been impressed by the British, and he knew she was worried about her family.

Becky shook her head. He could see the sorrow in her eyes as she turned to face him. "How I wish we knew where my father is. I guess he's still on that British ship. Mother is so sad and she works so hard. Sam is such a big help I don't know what she would do without him. I'm glad to be working at the Pratt's so I can help with money."

"Who knows, maybe this durn war will be over soon. Your father will come home and your mother can stop worrying." Austin patted her shoulder.

"I pray for that every day. But now, let's talk about some good things happening like a picnic next Sunday," said Becky with a twinkle in her eye. The Pratt's roast a chicken every Sunday and there is always plenty left, so I'll bring some chicken and I'll make a dessert, but don't ask what. I'll surprise you."

They continued to walk slowly and finally arrived at the Pratt home. After saying goodby and while Austin was walking back to his house, he thought about how easy it was to talk with Becky. He could say anything and she always listened so intently.

The week passed quickly and Sunday was another beautiful day. Austin and Becky meandered along the road out of town. He knew the best place to have a picnic. When he and Beth and sometimes Nate had a chance to play when they were younger, they had discovered a special place. Outside of town, there was a grove of evergreen trees and a small pond. Sometimes they pretended they were Indians. They would make teepees out of twigs and build tiny rafts to float on the pond. Yep, that was a great place for a picnic. He carried the picnic basket and had brought a blanket, so they could sit down to eat their lunch. It didn't take them very long to finish the chicken and enjoy a very large piece of chocolate cake, Becky's surprise dessert. They shared the milk in the pail Becky had also brought with her. When they finished eating, they sat on the rocks beside the pond. Among the lily pads, they spotted several heads of frogs patiently waiting for an unsuspecting insect.

"I think the insects have decided it's too cold for them," laughed Austin. "Bout time those frogs find themselves a home at the bottom of the pond, 'cause it sure has plenty of mud."

"Try to catch one. There's a big bullfrog right in front of you, Austin," Becky cried. "Can you catch it?"

Austin kneeled down and slowly moved his hands closer and closer to the bullfrog. With one mighty leap, the bullfrog disappeared into the dark water. "By golly, he was quick. Don't think I'll catch any frogs today. It's getting late but we have time to go to the shipyard," Austin suggested. "Bet you've never been up close to all the ships we're building." Austin was proud of the job the men were doing, and wanted Becky to be impressed by all the ships. Besides, he could explain the differences among the various ships, and he could show her the ones he had helped build. They quickly packed up the remains of their lunch and folded the blanket. It didn't take very long to reach the shipyard.

It was late afternoon and no one seemed to be around. As Austin explained about the type of vessels there and also his part in the building of them, he happened to glance toward the road.

"Becky, look over there. See that man standing on the road? I've seen him a couple of times staring over here at the shipyard. He seems to be checking on how many ships are here and how many are finished. My father and the other workers wonder if he is a spy for the British. No one seems to know who he is, so he can't live here in town. But he sure acts suspicious."

Becky was staring at the man. "I think I've seen that man before. Yes, I'm pretty sure he lives in a shack near the lighthouse in Saybrook. I don't know his name. When I see my brother, I'll describe him and maybe Sam will know who he is. Better yet I'll write Sam a letter. Oh look Austin, he sees us watching him."

The man abruptly turned and hurried down the road where he had tied his horse to a tree. Quickly he jumped into the saddle and disappeared down the road.

"Look at him go. Bet he didn't expect to see anyone at the shipyard. When I get home I'll tell my father I saw that man again. Guess we'd better be going. I'll walk you back to the Pratt's. Guess they'll be looking for you."

They strolled along the road until they reached the Pratt home and walked around to the back door.

"That sure was fun, Becky. Glad we could have a picnic and the cake was sure good." Austin shuffled his feet. "Uh, would you like to walk out with me again?" He said knowing he was blushing.

She paused and lightly touched his hand. "I'd like

that, Austin. We had fun today. Best I go in though, before Mrs. Pratt wonders where I am. I'll write to Sam tomorrow about that man we saw at the shipyard. Hope he knows who he is. Sam is bringing my winter clothes sometime next week and no doubt he'll stop to see you and let you know about that man.

"That will be great to see Sam. Well, guess I'd better get home. Bye, Becky, we sure did have fun." He waved, and felt he was walking on air on the way home. I think Becky likes me, he thought.

His mother was in the kitchen with Beth. They had just finished washing the dishes. Beth turned around as Austin walked in and smiled at him.

"Looks like you had fun on your picnic with Becky. You're grinning from ear to ear. Look at Austin, Ma."

His mother laughed. "Yep, it sure does look like a big grin. But now that you're back, Austin, I want you to bring in a couple of armfuls of firewood, and you had better take care of the horses and cows. Molly hasn't been milked yet. Get Nate to help you."

Ten days later, Austin heard Grandfather talking with someone out by the barn. The family had finished breakfast, and Austin and Nate were ready to go outside to help their grandfather and take care of the livestock.

"Hey Nate, I bet that's Sam. Sure sounds like his voice." The door banged as Austin hurried out to the barn. "Sam, You're up early. Did you bring Becky's winter clothes? Did you get the letter she sent? Do you know the man she wrote about in her letter?"

"Yep, brought the clothes and yep, I know the man." Sam dismounted and came over to shake Austin's hand.

"Can't stay too long. I have to give Becky her clothes and get home so I can help my ma."

"Let me get my father. I know he wants to hear about this strange man."

"I'm right here," his father called from the barn. He was carrying the pitchfork. He had been pitching hay into the horse stalls. He dropped the pitchfork as he hurried over to the boys. "So tell us about this man, Sam."

"He lives in a shack near the lighthouse and he has a bunch of children. I know his wife takes in washing, but I don't think he works. His name is Jeremiah Glover. Apparently he borrows money from some of the folks and never pays them back. Everyone is wise to him now, and his money source has dried up. People don't think much of him."

"Appreciate your telling us about this man, Sam. I'm going to tell the other men at work what you said, and we'll all watch for him. Do you have time to come in for some breakfast?" Mr. Lay said, as he patted Sam's horse.

"Thanks Mr. Lay, but I'd better be going." He mounted his horse, and waved goodbye.

Austin yelled at him as Sam started down the road. "Tell Becky I said hello."

His father then picked up his pitchfork and hurried to the barn. "Come on, Austin, we have work to do. I'm sure glad Sam stopped and told us about this man. He sounds sneaky. Could be the British hired him to spy on the shipyard."

# CHAPTER7

## CHRISTMAS HOLIDAYS-1813

It was a cold winter. It snowed and snowed. Grandfather and Austin had to dig a path to the barn almost every day. As soon as the path was cleared, snow would fall the next day, and they would start all over again. It was necessary to take care of the livestock. They also had to dig paths to the chicken coop and the well.

Several days before Christmas, Austin, Nate, and their father put on their heavy coats and hats, their winter boots and their gloves. Taking a hatchet and saw from the shed, they were ready to search for a Christmas tree in the woods outside of town. They trudged through the snow while Nate would say, "I like that tree, No, that one over there is better."

Their father burst out laughing. "Nate, we haven't even gotten to the woods yet. You'll see plenty of trees there, but only one will come home with us, so just wait and choose one when we get there."

The wind had picked up and it was mighty cold. They

wanted to find a tree quickly, cut it down and hurry home to a warm fire. "That's the one," shouted Nate, "over there." No one argued with his choice. It was a beautiful hemlock with snow laden branches that gracefully bowed and swayed. It didn't take them very long to cut down the tree and drag it home. No one spoke on the way home. They were all thinking of a warm fire and some hot cider.

"Ma, we have the tree," yelled Nate, "and it's a beauty."

"Landsake, you all look so cold and your faces are so red they look like red apples. Hurry, take off your boots and sit by the fire. Beth, get some hot cider for them so they can thaw out."

Beth and Mary were anxious to decorate the tree. They had dried orange and lemon slices and tied them with red ribbon. They would look so lovely hanging on the branches. Nate had strings of berries to wind around the tree. When they were finished decorating, they all stood back to admire their beautiful tree.

Everyone had secretly been making gifts. Mrs. Lay had frantically been knitting scarves and mittens for the family. When all were asleep, she would creep down the stairs, put another log on the fire, sit in her favorite chair and knit, knit, knit. Mr. Lay spent hours in the barn along with Grandfather building wooden boxes for everyone to use for their special treasures. Grandfather had also made new fishing poles for Austin and Nate.

Christmas Eve they walked to church. The snow covered roads had ruts caused by the wagons and carriages.

Everyone found it was easier to follow the ruts than to struggle through the deep snow. When they were walking home, Austin turned to his mother. "I talked to Becky when we were leaving church and she won't be able to go home. I invited her to come for dinner tomorrow. I didn't think you'd mind."

"Of course not. We'll be glad to see her and I made an extra pair of mittens so you can wrap them to give to her. Then she'll have a gift to open, too."

Dinner was grand. Mr. Lay had shot a wild turkey and Mrs. Lay and the girls had been busy in the kitchen all morning, making delicious vegetable dishes and desserts. After dinner, while Mr. and Mrs. Lay and Grandfather rested, the young people wrapped themselves in their new scarves and mittens. The snow was still falling, and a perfect time to have a snowball fight. No one escaped. By the time it was getting dark, they were all covered with snow.

That evening Austin and Beth walked Becky back to the Pratt's home. It had been a very satisfying Christmas.

# CHAPTER 8

# THE BRITISH RAID

APRIL 8, 1814

Captain Richard Coote, part of the blockade force off New London, checked his orders again. He was to lead a raiding party on the shipyards located six miles up the Connecticut River. They were now in Long Island Sound near the mouth of the river. He had been told that the fort and lighthouse were not guarded. He ordered his first mate to drop anchor and signal the other three sloops to drop anchor. The townspeople of the small village of Saybrook, located at the mouth of the river, were no doubt sleeping as there were no lights. It was April 7th and a brisk wind was blowing.

The crews on all four sloops were commanded to be completely quiet as sounds carried on the water. Captain Coote could dimly see the coastline near the mouth of the river. It was approximately 9:45 P.M. and he was getting anxious. Where was the turncoat, Mr. Glover? He should be coming aboard by now. Suddenly there was a faint scraping sound near the water line and looking down from the deck, he could see a figure climbing up the ladder. Well, he had finally arrived. He'd better have the chart showing the channel up the river, he thought, as the turncoat's head appeared. He was going to be polite to this spy, but nevertheless, he found his actions contemptible.

Mr. Glover did have the chart. After studying the chart in his cabin by an oil lamp, Captain Coote gave orders to the other brigs. One of the brigs was to remain there to provide cover if needed upon their return. Six shallow-draft boats were lowered from the brigs with one hundred and thirty six British marines aboard with many cannonades, and rifles with bayonets. They also carried torches, and plenty of lines and hooks, all the equipment needed for a hit and run surprise landing party.

All this preparation took several hours. When they were ready, they rowed up the river as quietly as possible. Not until sometime after 3 A.M. on April 8th did the British arrive at the shipyard.

Captain Coote had taken the turncoat in his boat. Immediately upon arriving at the village, Mr. Glover hid in the bottom of the boat.

A horseman had spotted the British boats rowing up the river, and raced to Essex to alert the townspeople. As the boats landed, townfolks opened fire with the few rifles they owned, and one four pounder, all the weaponry they had.

Captain Coote ordered his men to return the fire. Seeing that they couldn't defend themselves against the barrage aimed at them, the residents ceased firing. By now everyone in town was awake. Many huddled together along the main road across from the shipyard.

The British marines marched over to where the townspeople were standing. An officer read a proclamation to them, stating the marines would be burning all the ships but would not harm or burn the village as long as no one would interfere. The people stood silently as the British sailors scurried from one ship to another getting them ready to go up in flames.

It took many hours for the British sailors to move the ships ready to be launched into the river and set them afire. The ships still under construction were torched in the shipyard.

Captain Coote stood by and directed the proceedings. The British officers collected information. They wrote down the name of each ship, the tonnage, how many guns, and whether they were outfitted as privateers.

In the meantime, Americans were riding to New London, Westbrook, and Killingsworth to alert their citizens of the danger. The militia gathered on each side of the river near the river's mouth. They hoped to bottle the British there to prevent them from escaping to their ships in the Sound.

For hours the people stood there stunned with tears running down their faces. All their hard work for naught. They were helpless, as they stood there watching the ships they had built going down in flames. Austin felt numb as he watched the destruction. Then he saw the British climb the ladder on the OSAGE and knew it would shortly be in flames. He couldn't let that happen. It was the largest vessel in the shipyard. It was almost ready to be launched and he had been so proud of the deck he had painted.

Quickly he dodged in back of everyone standing there, and dashed across the road to the far side of the shipyard where the OSAGE was located. He knew there was a ladder on each side of the ship. He quickly climbed the ladder that was on the side where the British couldn't see him. When he reached the deck, he saw that the British had already torched the cabin. Darting behind them, he grabbed one of the vats of water and tried to douse the flames. His face was black with soot, except where tears had made small rivers down his cheeks. He grabbed another vat and just as he was about to throw that water on the flames, he heard a yell.

"Hey there, boy, what do you think you're doing?" One of the British sailors cuffed his head, grabbed his arms, and hollered to another sailor, "Bring those chains over here. I got me a prisoner!"

Austin struggled but to no avail. One of the British sailors threw Austin over his shoulder, climbed down the ladder and then forced him to walk towards one of the British boats, where his legs were also chained. He was thrown to the bottom of the boat and his leg chains were then tied to the boat. "Well there, boy, a fine kettle of fish you're in now. But just you wait. It's going to get a lot worse." The sailor smirked.

Mr. Lay was watching every move the British made, when suddenly he saw a lad being forced across the shipyard towards one of their boats. "Oh dear lord, it's Austin. They've captured him. He's a prisoner!"

Wilbur Cooper was standing close to Mr. Lay. "So that's who it is. I thought I saw a lad on the OSAGE, but I didn't know it was Austin. He must have tried to put out the flames. What can we do?"

"If I get my hands on one of those British, I know what I'll do." Mr. Lay was frantically rubbing his hands together. He was ready to burst with anger, but he was completely helpless.

When all the vessels were destroyed, the Marines marched back to their boats. By this time, Captain Coote figured they would be attacked by local militia. The destruction of the ships had taken many hours. There had been plenty of time for the Americans to plan an ambush. Rowing back to their boats anchored in the Sound would be dangerous. He expected them to attack from both sides of the river and try to bottle them up before they could reach their brigs anchored in the Sound.

Austin was trembling so hard he was making his chains rattle. Not that anyone would hear him. He had heard Captain Coote order his men to keep their eyes open and be ready to be attacked.

Suddenly bullets were flying overhead. The boom of cannons and the shouts of both the British and Americans forced him to try to be as small as possible. Never had Austin been so frightened. He heard a British sailor cry out, and then he saw him fall overboard. He had been shot.

It took the British until late morning to finally reach their brigs. Two of their men had been killed, but otherwise their mission had been a success.

As they all hurried aboard and were ready to sail, Austin was dragged in front of Captain Coote. "Well what do we have here? The only brave person in the whole town? What did you plan to do? Take on all our Marines and sailors? What's your name?" Captain Coote demanded.

Austin could barely speak. His voice croaked. "Austin Lay sir, uh, Captain."

Captain Coote had a very stern look. "You were gutsy. young man. I could take you as a prisoner, and keep you in chains, but you were the only one brave enough to take on the British Navy, so I have decided to let you go. Before we set sail, your chains will be removed and you'll be thrown overboard. I hope you can swim. Yonder is the shore."

A reprieve. Austin gulped. Yes, he could swim and he would make it to shore. The chains were removed and a husky sailor picked him up. "There you go, lad," he yelled as he threw him overboard.

Austin hit the water hard, and for a moment he was stunned. He started to flounder. He would need all his strength to get to the shore. He began to swim towards the lighthouse. If he kept that in sight, he would make it. The British brigs were already sailing away. He was alone in the cold water. Now he needed to concentrate on getting to shore.

# CHAPTER 9

## SINK OR SWIM

The water was so cold, and he knew he had to keep swimming or he would drown. He had used every last ounce of his strength as he reached land. He lay there exhausted, and shivering in his wet clothes. When he had gained back his strength, he stood up, and realized he was close to the Larson's home. Hurrying as fast as possible, he finally arrived. He knocked and knocked.

"It's me, Austin. Help," he shouted.

He heard Mrs. Larson, "Hold on Austin, I'll be right there." When she opened the door, he stumbled inside.

"Landsakes, you're soaking wet and shivering. Sam," she called, "get some dry clothes and a blanket. Austin's here, and he's soaked to the skin. Get over here by the fire, Austin. I'll make some hot cider for you." She put some more logs on the fire and bright flames sprung up. Austin moved as close to the fire as possible. Sam rushed in with some of his clothes and a blanket.

"Get out of those wet clothes, Austin, and when

you're ready, tell us what happened. By this time the whole family gathered around him. The hot cider was warming his insides, and he was finally getting warm. As he sipped the cider, he told them what had happened. "And that Mr. Glover who lives here in Saybrook is a spy! He was on Captain Coote's sloop." Austin's teeth were still chattering.

"As soon as you're up to it, I'll take you home. We can ride double on ole Bucky," said Sam. "Your family will sure be glad to see you. Golly, they probably think you're still a prisoner or maybe even dead."

Austin was finally warm, and soon the two boys were on their way.

In the meantime, aboard Captain Coote's sloop the BORER, Glover appeared, groveling in front of the captain. "If you please, Captain, I'd like the rest of my money. You paid me $1000 dollars and owe me another $1000 dollars."

Captain Coote looked at Mr. Glover with disgust. Abruptly, he turned, strode to his cabin and returned with the money in a sack. He dropped it on the deck. "There's your money. Pick it up. Men, lower this man's rowboat and get him off of here."

As Mr. Glover started rowing as fast as he could, the men heard Captain Coote mutter, "I despise turncoats."

It was late afternoon when Sam and Austin arrived in Essex. Nate saw them coming and rushed inside. "It's Austin, he's back. He's here with Sam," he yelled. The family rushed outside to greet him.

Mrs. Lay started to cry and wiped her eyes on her

apron. "Oh, Austin, we thought we'd never see you again."

She hugged him as Mr. Lay was patting his shoulder. Nate was hugging him around his knees, while Beth and Mary grinned from ear to ear.

Nate wasn't the only one to see Sam and Austin ride into town. Some of the neighbors also saw them and ran around telling everyone the good news that Austin was back. It didn't take long before all the people gathered in front of the Lay's house.

Mr. Cooper spoke up. "All of us are so thankful that you are safe and home with your family. We all know what you tried to do and you are our hero." Everyone clapped and shouted, "Hurrah for Austin." Mr. Cooper continued. "What happened to you? The last we saw of you was in chains and carried aboard one of the British longboats." The people waited expectedly to hear Austin's story.

Austin looked around at all the people he knew and almost choked up. They were all so concerned for him that he could feel his eyes watering, just a bit.

"I'll tell you what happened." The people listened to his story and realized how brave he was. When he was finished his tale, he said, "Captain Coote was a real gentleman, and golly, I'm sure glad he let me go."

Becky was in the crowd listening. When he was finished, she rushed up to him. "I'm so glad you're safe and well. You are my hero!" She lightly kissed him on the cheek, and blushing, she ran back through the crowd and disappeared.

Austin looked dazed as his father put his arm around

him. "Look, here comes your grandfather. He's been out in the skiff looking for you."

"I heard Becky say you were her hero. You're my hero, too," said Grandfather with a big grin.

Mr. Lay laughed. "We have to get Austin inside. I'm sure he's starved, and he needs to rest. Thank all of you for your concern about my son. We were all so worried, but now he's safe and back with us."

Later, when Austin was in bed, he thought about all that had happened. The last two days had been a harrowing experience and he would never forget. Best of all, Becky had kissed him. That was his last thought before he fell asleep.

# EPILOGUE

The war was not over. Some important events happened after the tragedy in Connecticut. Four months later on August 24,1814, the British invaded Washington, DC. They were successful in defeating the American troops that were guarding the capitol. A flag of truce was sent, stating only public buildings would be torched. Washington had practically been abandoned. The American troops had vanished and President Madison and his wife, Dolly had also left the city. Although the city had been the seat of government for fourteen years, little progress had been made. The British burned the Washington Navy Yard, the Capitol, Library of Congress and of course the White House. Our capital had been set aflame.

One month later, the British sailed up the Patapsco River to Baltimore. Their fleet consisted of seventeen vessels including five bomb and rocket boats. The city was twelve miles up the river, and Fort McHenry was located on the point overlooking the narrow entrance to the harbor.

Francis Scott Key, a young lawyer was on a truce ship in the harbor, negotiating a release of a prisoner. This man happened to be a friend of the President. The bombardment by the British made it impossible to leave the ship. The bombs and rockets continued through the night. On the morning of September 14, he was amazed to see our flag still flying over Fort McHenry. It was then that Francis Scott Key was so moved to see the American troops had overcome the enemy, he wrote a poem. This was eventually set to music, and became our National Anthem.

In December of 1814, the British and American negotiators signed the Treaty of Ghent, which took place in Belgium. This should have been the end of the war.

But in January of 1815, the battle of New Orleans occurred. The British had a navy of more than fifty ships that sailed from Jamaica transporting ten thousand troops.

Upon receiving this information, Major General Andrew Jackson arrived in the city and began preparing fortifications, which were mostly built of mud and bales of hay.

The English Armada was able to find an accessible waterway nine miles from the city and then advanced to the outskirts of New Orleans. Jackson quickly launched a nighttime surprise attack with his four thousand men. His "army" consisted of some frontiersmen, former slaves, and the famous pirate Jean Lafitte and his men. This brave group of men defeated the British.

The war was officially over on February 17, 1815. The Congress had ratified the Treaty of Ghent.

# MORE INFORMATION

The British Raid on the Essex shipyards delivered a devastating blow on the American forces. America desperately needed those twenty eight vessels and the Essex shipyards destroyed by the British. It is unlikely, however, you will find any information concerning this raid in American history books. Why? Two reasons have been given. First, the success of the raid was extremely embarrassing to the Connecticut militia in the area because its members had not guarded the fort at the mouth of the Connecticut River nor had they insured that the Saybrook lighthouse was adequately manned. Thus the British were successful in accomplishing what they had set out to do. Second, and perhaps more important in the suppression of the British raid, some of the important citizens of Essex, including one of the owners of the shipyards, knew the Governor of Connecticut rather well. Among themselves they decided the less known of the British victory, the better off they and the state of Connecticut would be. Silence saved embarrassment and also might improve morale among the citizens.

Information concerning the raid can be found in two important sources.

Latimer, Jon. The 1812 War with America. Cambridge, Massachusetts: Belknap Press, 2007.

Jon Latimer is an English historian and has utilized the British naval archives as well as American archives. On page 247 of his study of the war, told primarily from the English, not the American, point of view, describes the raid on the Essex shipyards by Captain Richard Coote.

Anderson, Russell F. The British Raid in Essex:

April 8,1814 research by Albert Dock, Essex Historical society, Inc.,1981.

Captain Anderson, USNR. And Commander Dock USNR., provide the most detail about the British raid on the Essex shipyards.

This pamphlet can be obtained through Donald Malcarne, Essex town historian at the Essex Historical Society, Essex, CT 06426.

# EDUCATIONAL STUDIES

1. Why was the War of 1812 called the second War of Independence?
2. Who was president during the war of 1812? Name his wife and find out what she was able to save before the White House was burned.
3. Describe one of the battles at sea between the British and the Americans. What ships were involved, how long the battle, who won, and did any famous saying occur?
4. Name three famous Americans and describe their importance during the war.
5. Imagine living in 1812. What would your life be like? What would a typical day be like back then? Pretend you lived on a farm or in town.
6. Describe the life of an impressed American on a British ship.
7. Look at a map showing the Great Lakes. Why did Americans decide they couldn't afford to lose Lake Ontario, but were not as concerned about losing Lake Erie?
8. What were the major fighting areas?

9. Why did Francis Scott Key write the Star Spangled Banner?
10. The Battle of New Orleans was the last battle. Why was it? Who was Jean Lafitte? Write a story about him as a pirate.
11. Write a story about Austin Lay. What do you think happened to the shipyard after the British raid?

# About the Author

Kajsa C. Cook, a former teacher, is a graduate of Pennsylvania State University. She lives in Pennsylvania and is the author of DISCOVERIES in the SHRIVER FAMILY ATTIC, a story about the Battle of Gettysburg. She is active in the Adams County Arts Council. She has three sons and seven grandchildren.

Essex was a busy small town in 1812. The town, then called Potopaug after an Indian tribe, was located six miles up the Connecticut River from the Long Island Sound. The town's main business was shipbuilding and many vessels were ready to fight against the British Navy and the embargo it forced upon the Americans

The British had heard about the ships waiting to be launched and were determined to prevent this from happening. Was there a spy who told the British?

Austin was a young lad who worked at the shipyard. One night he became the town hero, but he was captured by the British during his valiant struggle to thwart their attempts to destroy the twenty- eight ships. It was a dark night for the town's residents.